Tide Pool
Tales

By Elaine Little

With Illustrations

By Bob Little

Tide Pool Tales

By Elaine Little

First Edition

Published by Robert L. Little
Sacramento, California

When ocean tides go wandering

The tide pool creatures stay

In a little home – just theirs alone

Beside the salty bay.

Here minnows grab at floating food

Or tiny things that squire

And any star fish could predict

The life span of a worm.

Anemones all open

With shell fish by their side

Await the surging of the sea;

The turning of the tide.

Swirling, tumbling come the waves

Each with a gusty motion

They bring to quiet tide pools

Tall tales from the ocean.

Inky, the kid, was a no-account squid

A rude unmannerly little squid kid

When sociable fish came to take him places

To fan fare frolics or octopus races,

What do you think that naughty squid did?

Squirted ink inn their faces.

Science fact:

When squids are alarmed or disturbed they squirt out an ink like fluid.

Debbil fish! Debbil fish!

Spare dat pinkling crab!

He's da only crusty one,

Sprawling, Brawling, lusty one

His crabby mother had.

Debbil fish! Debbil fish!

Jest nibble off a claw!

He can grow another one,

A spinkin, spankin, other one

To please his crabby ma.

Science fact:

A favorite food of the devil ray is small crustaceans.

Funny flat flounder

With two right eyes,

Both on one side of his head,

He changes his color as a disguise

Gray or brown or red.

Science fact:

Within a few days after a flounder has been hatched one eye starts
moving to the opposite side of the head.

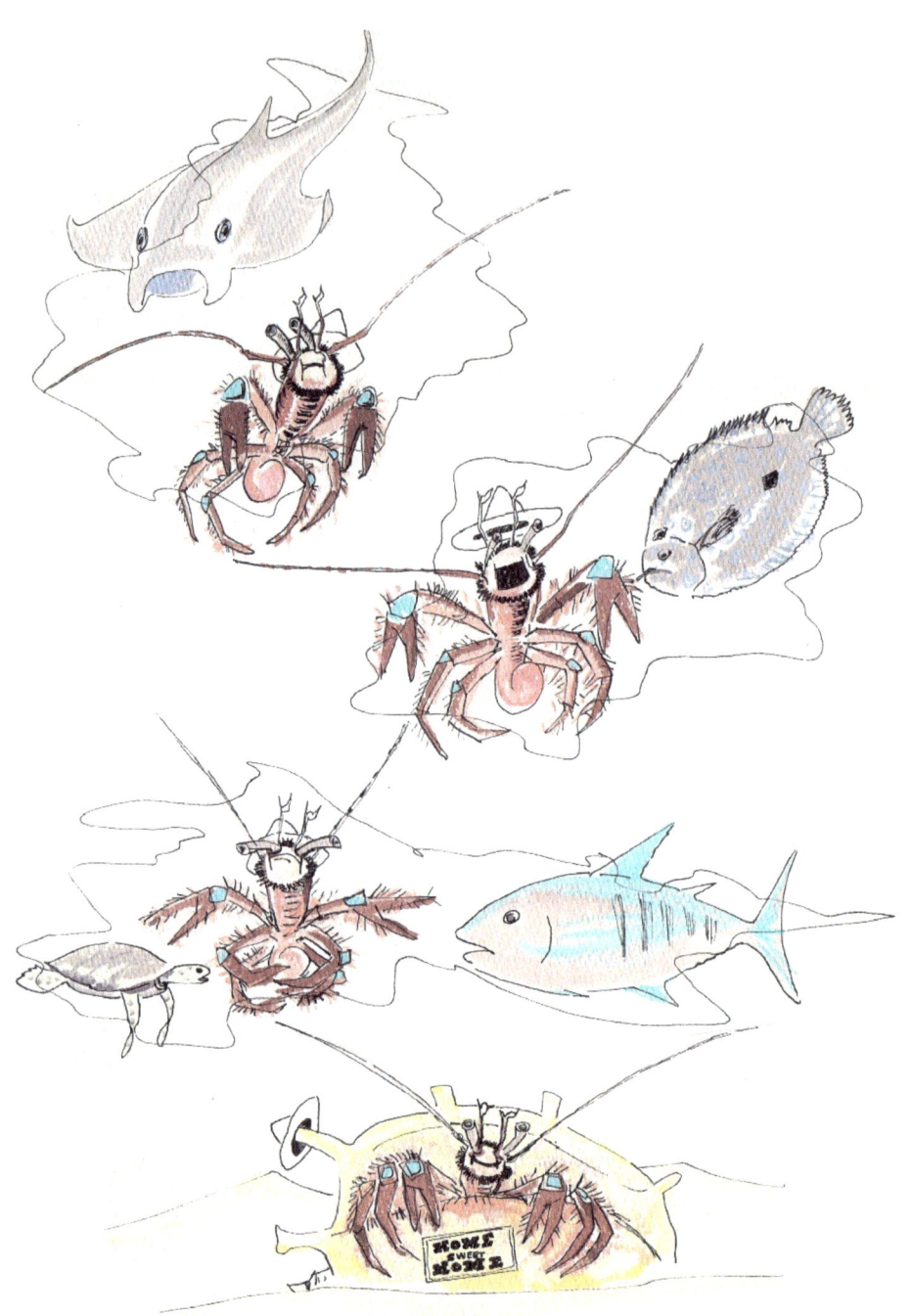

Kermit, the hermit crab had no home

No secret hide-away of his own

He was chased by devil rays

Bit by flounders

Teased by turtles

And blue fin bounders.

When Happy Kermit found a shell

Where some poor shell fish used to dwell.

Curved and canopied,

Polished, shining!

He moved right in and started dining.

Science fact:

Hermit crabs find empty shells to live in when they grow too large
for one shell, they find another.

South of Bermuda

In the warm Sargasso sea

Lived an old mother eel

And her little eels three.

"Swim away," said the mother,

"We swim," said the three.

So they swam far away,

From the Sargasso sea.

Thru the cold Atlantic

In lakes and rivers new

Seven long years,

Those elf eels grew.

Then, when it was time,

To raise a family,

Back they swam two thousand miles

To the warm Sargasso sea.

Science fact:

Eels,. like salmon return to their birthplace to spawn.

An octo named Gust,

Had no one he could trust

So he hid in dark ink clouds around him.

But hoo-ray! One bright day,

In spite of the spray,

A pretty miss octopus found him.

Science fact:

Both octopus and the squid squirt out an inky fluid as a protection.

Black Angler with lighted Antenna

Your time clock, tides of the sea.

Which channel is best,

For your maritime guest,

When tuning in on Sea V?

Science fact:

The lighted antenna of the black angler lures small fish into its
wide open mouth.

"Listen little shellies",

Said an oyster mother,

"You better be good to one another!

"That old brown sea weed up overhead,

"Snatches naughty oysters

"Right out of their bed!"

Science fact:

A certain variety of seaweed has suction cups.

They can fasten these on an oyster, draw it up, and absorb it.

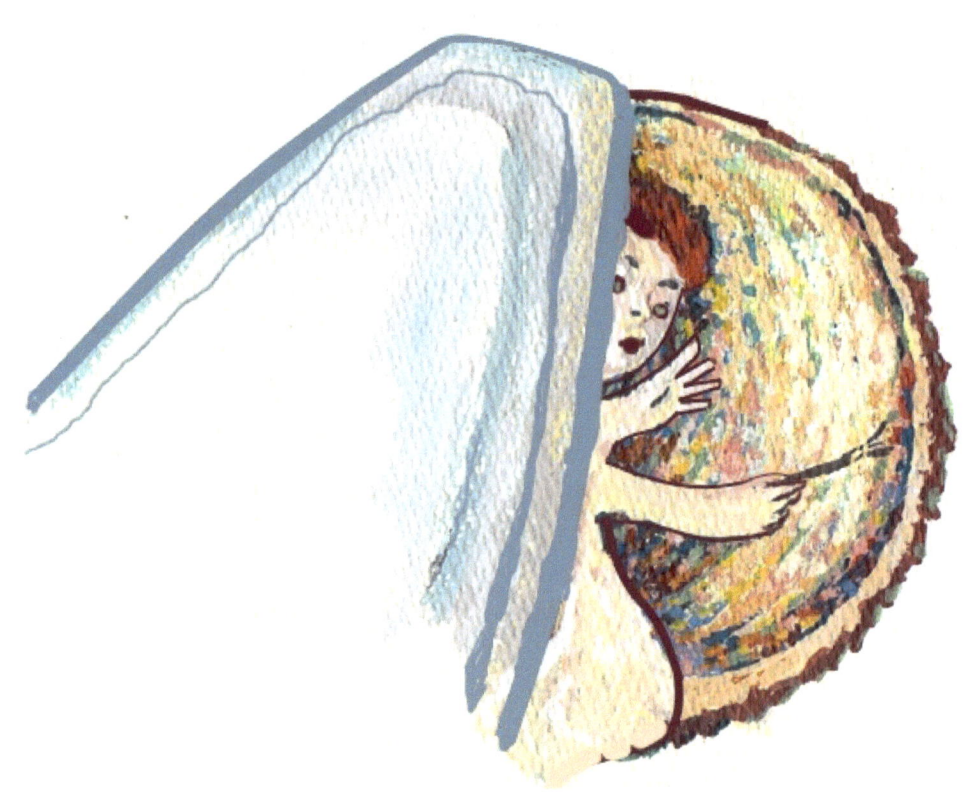

Abalone clings to the rock,

Guards with his life,

A rare rainbow.

Abalone may never tell,

What dream has etched,

And painted his shell

With live translucent glow.

Science fact:

The abalone is made into delicious steaks. Its empty shell shines
with lovely colors.

A barnacle is attaché.

He builds his house,

On ships to stay,

And rears his family all around him.

You may scrape him off –

But cannot drown him.

'tho mighty gales shake up the ocean,

Bill Barnacle feels no commotion.

Science fact:

Barnacles are living creatures. They attach themselves to the bottoms and sides of ships in such numbers as to cause damage to many ships.

The flexible star fish

And frolicsome crab,

Wander about unafraid.

With faith as a grain of shining sand,

They never need first aid.

Said starfish bright to agile crab,

"Listen crusty brother,

"If you lose a pincer,

"Or I lose an arm,

"We can always grow another."

Science fact:

Both star fish and crabs have the ability to grow new limbs.

I wonder if bright angel fish

Are guardians of the blue,

Of lonesome seaweed babies

And silver minnows too.

When tiny fry are frightened

Perhaps they make a wish

And thru the waves quick as a splash,

Comes their guardian angel fish.

Science fact:

Angel fishes are noted for their beautiful colors.

Each fragile shell, remembers well,

The whispering sea's melodic rune.

Put a shell to your ear,

And the murmur you hear

Is a song of the tides and the moon.

Science fact:

The whispering sound you hear when you put your ear to a sea
shell come from the chambers in the shell.

Globigerina, slimy ooze

Carpets the ocean floor

Bones and skeletons two miles thick,

Of fishes that lived before.

In ages past were the trilobites,

Mollusks and starfish brittle

'Tis a kettle of very strange fish indeed!

That old sea bottom kettle.

Science fact:

Trilobites, mollusks and starfish were among the earliest forms of
life in the sea.

Portuguese Man Of War,

Shimmering fair

Floats in the briny deep.

Tentacles rare.

Curious trusting fishies

Are enchanted, caught, detained,

By stinging cells immobilized,

In living nets enchained,

Then from its galley, Portuguese,

This one-man navy

Serves chow deluxe, soup to nuts,

Including gravy.

Science fact:

The Portuguese man of war paralyzes its victims with the poison
stinging cells on its tentacles.

Sir Hippocampus, Sea Horse,

Equipped with incubator,

Hatches baby sea colts

In his pouch.

They squirm and disobey,

When papa says "Neigh, neigh.!"

So he quickly dumps them

From their cozy couch.

Ouch!

Science fact:

The generic name of the sea horse is Hippocampus, meaning horse
caterpillar.

The male sea horse hatches the eggs.

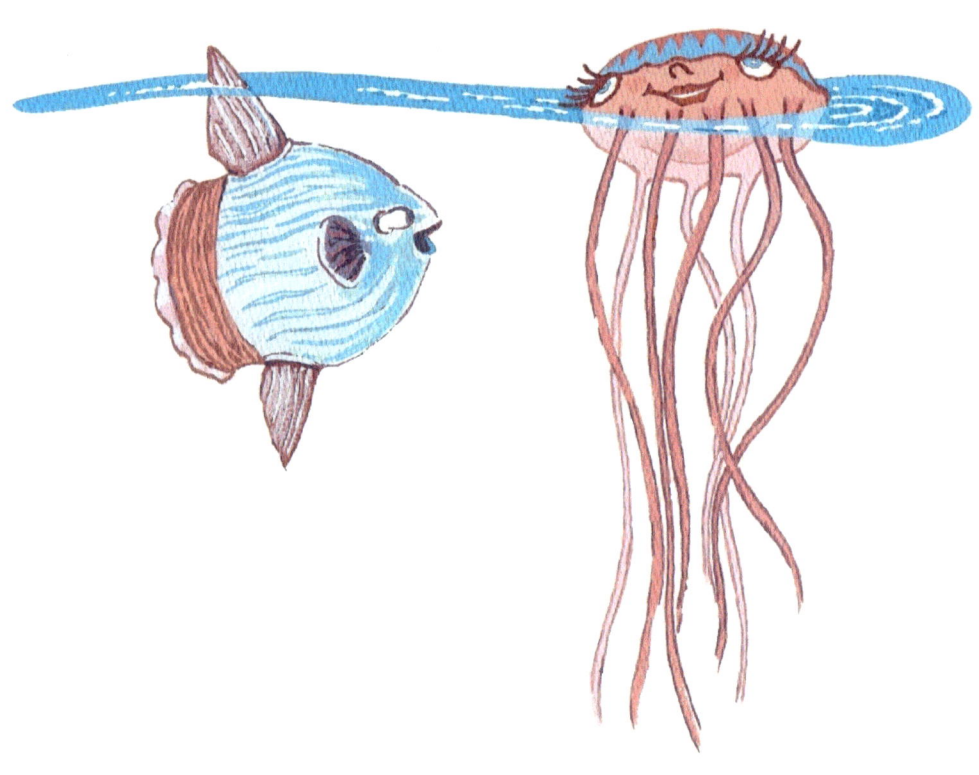

A flirtatious jelly fish

Called Dora Dummy
Was vainly proud
Of her pretty round tummy
Big Sol, the sun fish,
Who never could diet,
Said "Wow what a sweet dish!
I really must try it"
At first he just nibbled,
Then swallowed D. Dummy.
Where is she now?
Way down in his tummy
Yummy, Yummy!

Science fact:

The gigantic ocean sunfish often weighing more than a ton has a
favorite food item – jelly fish.

The author

Elaine Little loved the sea and often spent her summers in Pacific Grove, California. She would rent a duplex near the sea and watch the ocean through a large window. Here, she would write poetry and imagine the creature of the sea as though they were her children.

Her two books about the sea, *Mother Goose in a Bathysphere* and *Tide Pool Tales*, were never published during her lifetime. With this publication both books are now available to the public.